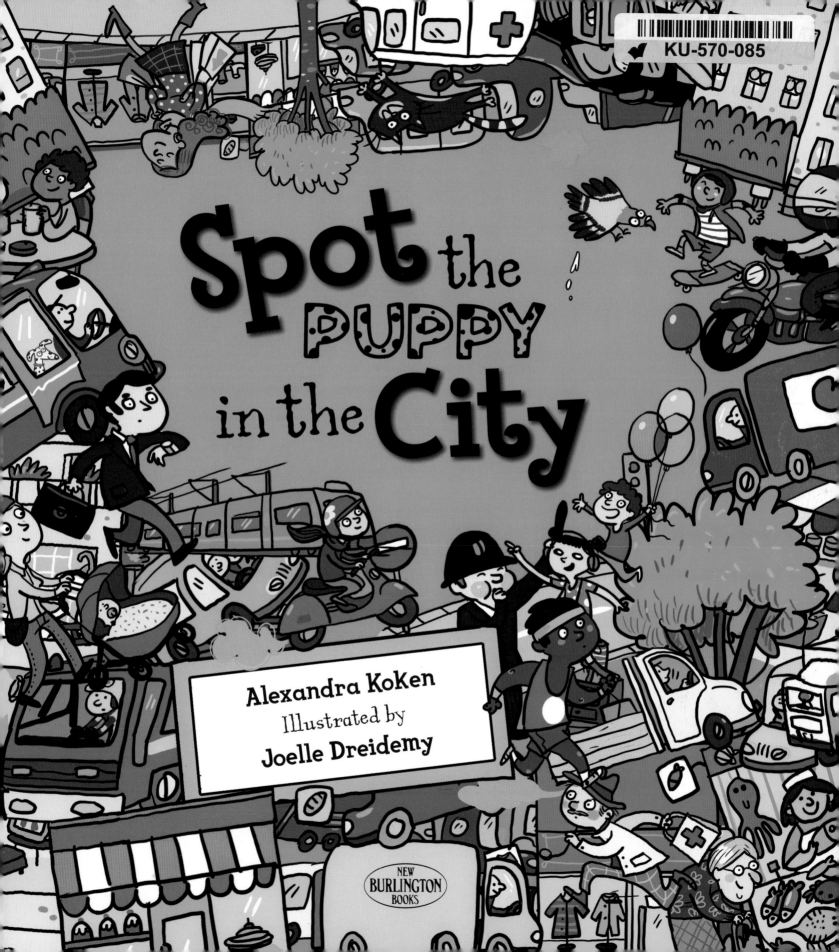

Spot the PUPPY in the City

Alexandra Koken

Illustrated by
Joelle Dreidemy

NEW BURLINGTON BOOKS

More people live in Tokyo, Japan, than in any other city in the world.

Can you spot these things?

banana skin   bucket   salad   clock   axe

Fire engines have sirens and flashing lights so people know to move out of the way.

Can you spot these things?

stripy kite   teddy bear   basket

lily pad   bin   ice cream

The longest ever traffic jam was almost as long as 17 football pitches.

The world's biggest
shopping centre
is in Dubai, UAE, and
has 1200 shops!

Can you spot these things?

baseball cap · shoe · Triceratops · notebook · sign

More to spot

Go back and find these scenes in the book!

Did you find me?

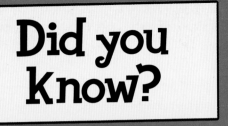

Did you Know?

One of the busiest airports in the world is in Atlanta, USA. One million planes take off from there every year.

In 1935, a man rode a bicycle around the world. He used seven sets of tyres.

The first department store opened in 1734.

The biggest T-rex skeleton is called 'Sue', and is kept in a museum in Chicago, USA.

The fastest road car can go at 430 kilometres per hour. That's almost four times as fast as a cheetah!

More city fun!

City visit

There are lots of great things to see in every city! Ask an adult to take you to a city near you, and visit some of the places in this book: a park, a museum or maybe a train station.

Hide and seek

Choose a cuddly toy that you can hide around your home for a friend or family member to spot, just like the puppy in this book! You could hide other objects and make a list of things to find.

Dream city

Draw your very own dream city. You can add anything you want! Is there a park? Or maybe a sports stadium? What would the buildings look like? Once you are happy with your sketch, you can colour it in and display it on your wall.

Apartment life

Using several different boxes stacked and glued together, make a block of flats like the ones in this book. Each box is a different flat where people live. Fill it with toy furniture and people, or make your own. You can rearrange them whenever you like!

A NEW BURLINGTON BOOK
The Old Brewery
6 Blundell Street
London N7 9BH

Designer: Krina Patel
Managing Editor: Victoria Garrard
Design Manager: Anna Lubecka

Copyright © QED Publishing 2013

First published in the UK in 2013
by QED Publishing

www.qed-publishing.co.uk

A catalogue record for this book is available from the British Library.

ISBN 978 1 78171 849 0

Printed in China